"A wonderful introduction to faithful women who served the Lord. These stories teach as they inspire. Your children will be blessed to learn about Corrie ten Boom's secret room."

MELISSA KRUGER, Author, *Wherever You Go, I Want You To Know*

"Laura Caputo-Wickham captures a big gospel for little hearts. The wonderful storytelling and charming illustrations make the mini-biographies in this series pitch-perfect for even the youngest readers."

CHAMP THORNTON, Author, *The Radical Book for Kids*

"This series brings to life the forgotten, teaches us valuable lessons, and imprints on us early on that if God kept our spiritual ancestors, he will keep us too."

K.A. ELLIS, Director, Edmiston Center for the Study of the Bible and Ethnicity

"A wonderful series, beautifully illustrated, introducing your children to godly women."

BLAIR LINNE, Spoken Word Artist

"Courage, intrigue, sacrifice and grief combined with a deep faith in Christ make Corrie's life an inspiration for parents and children alike. Imagine the impact this book could have on the next generation—it's like gospel dynamite!"

LINDA ALLCOCK, Author, *Head, Heart, Hands* and *Deeper Still*

"All of us, and children especially, love heroes and heroines. There is here a sense of adventure but also of high spiritual and moral purpose."

BISHOP MICHAEL NAZIR-ALI, President, Oxford Centre for Training, Research, Advocacy and Dialogue; Former Bishop of Rochester, UK

"Corrie ten Boom's life will impact your children and show them what it means to live for God."

BARBARA REAOCH, Author, *A Jesus Christmas* and *A Better Than Anything Christmas*

Corrie ten Boom
© Laura Caputo-Wickham / The Good Book Company 2021.
Reprinted 2021 (twice), 2022, 2024.

Illustrated by Isabel Muñoz | Design and Art Direction by André Parker

"The Good Book For Children" is an imprint of The Good Book Company Ltd
thegoodbook.com | thegoodbook.co.uk | thegoodbook.com.au
thegoodbook.co.nz | thegoodbook.co.in

ISBN: 9781784985783 | JOB-007685 | Printed in India

thegoodbook
for children

Do Great Things for God

Corrie ten Boom

The Courageous Woman and the Secret Room

Laura Caputo-Wickham

Illustrated by Isabel Muñoz

Corrie ten Boom lived in a higgledy-piggledy house, surrounded by family, friends and LOTS of clocks...

There were tall clocks,
   tiny clocks,
fancy clocks,
   and funny clocks.

And Father, the finest
clockmaker in the Dutch
city of Haarlem, knew
how to fix them all!

Corrie's family met together every day to read the Bible.

"You are my hiding place and my shield," read Father one day. "I hope in your word."*

*Psalm 119 v 114

Corrie sat there, wondering,

"Why would anybody need a hiding place?"

The answer came many years later.

Corrie was sleeping in her room when a
loud **BANG!** woke her up.
As she looked outside, she saw brilliant
flashes followed by booming explosions.

"War," she whispered.

It was indeed war. A big one, called World War Two. Countries were fighting, and people were bullied and killed for how they looked or talked, or where they came from.

Some of these people were Jews.

They were chased by the soldiers and put into horrible prison camps where many died.

As Corrie watched this happening, she prayed a very brave prayer.

"Lord Jesus, I give myself for the Jewish people. In any way. Any place. Any time."

And just as with every prayer prayed by a follower of Jesus, this too was heard.

Soon, Corrie found herself part of a top-secret group that helped to hide as many Jews as possible.

She had to cycle to secret meetings in the middle of the night.

And hide important documents in
her father's clock shop.

She even had a secret room
built inside her bedroom!

Hundreds of Jews came and went from her house,
as Corrie helped them to find a safer home.
Every so often, they had practice drills. They
would pretend that the soldiers had arrived, and
everybody had to hide in less than one minute!

Then, one night, the soldiers came,
and this time it was not a drill.

Loud, angry men searched every corner of the house, slamming doors, kicking chairs and tipping things over.

But they didn't find the secret room.

Corrie and her family, though, were taken to prison.

Life in the prison camp was terrible. Corrie had to work in the freezing cold; she had to sleep in beds full of lice, and all she had to eat was cold, gloopy food.

It could have been easy for Corrie to feel completely and utterly hopeless. But she didn't...

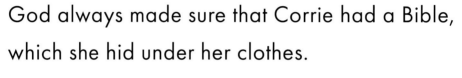

God always made sure that Corrie had a Bible,
which she hid under her clothes.

Whenever she read it, she found hope and courage.

She learned to forgive even when it was hard, and
to find joy in the small things—even the lice!

Soon, other prisoners joined Corrie and her
sister, Betsie, in reading the Bible and praying.
Many of them trusted in Jesus as their King.

Corrie's trust in God gave her the strength to go on until the day she was finally free to go home. From then on, Corrie talked about her life to big crowds, saying, *"There's no pit so deep that God's love is not deeper still"*.

Corrie knew that very well.

You are my hiding place and my shield;
I hope in your word
Psalm 119 v 114

Corrie ten Boom

1892 – 1983

"You are my hiding place and my shield."

Psalm 119 v 114

Questions to Think About

1. Which part of Corrie's story did you like best?

2. God's word, the Bible, was so important to Corrie that she hid a secret copy while she was in the prison camp and read it whenever she could. How important is the Bible to you? What can you do to show that?

3. In the prison camp, Corrie learned to find joy in small things—even the lice! The lice made the prison guards stay away, so that Corrie was free to read the Bible with other prisoners. Can you think of a "small thing", maybe even something you find hard, that God uses to help you?

4. What ideas does Corrie's story give you about how you might serve Jesus when you are older?

5. What is one truth about God that you'd like to remember from this story?

Corrie ten Boom

15th April 1892 Cornelia Arnolda Johanna ten Boom was born.

Her mother was also called Cornelia, and her father was Casper ten Boom, a renowned watchmaker in the city of Haarlem, in the Netherlands.

Corrie's family believed in God and read their family Bible together every day. Their faith inspired them to serve the people of their town in practical ways.

1921 By the age of 30, Corrie was helping her father in his shop. She became the first woman licensed as a watchmaker in the Netherlands.

In 1940, the Germans invaded the Netherlands, and many Jewish people were in danger. They were arrested and sent to horrible prisons called concentration camps. Corrie and her family opened their house to help as many Jews as possible to hide before starting a new life somewhere safer. Corrie played an important part in this. She cycled to secret meetings in the middle of the night and sneaked out important documents. She even had a secret room built inside her bedroom! The results were amazing. There was no way to tell that a tiny room was hidden behind the fake wall.

28 February 1944 Corrie's entire family was arrested and taken to prison. Some of Corrie's relatives were released, though her father didn't survive. Corrie and her sister, Betsie, were sent to a concentration camp in the Netherlands called Scheveningen and then to one in Germany called Ravensbrück. There, Corrie and her sister were forced to work all day in terrible conditions, and many of their fellow prisoners were killed.

On more than one occasion, though, Corrie was secretly given a Bible which she would read with Betsie, as well as sharing it with the other prisoners.

Thanks to Betsie's encouragement, Corrie learnt to be thankful for little things, including the lice in their beds. In fact, it was because of the lice that the guards stayed away from their room, giving them the freedom to meet and read the Bible.

Many women found courage in God's word, thanks to Corrie's and Betsie's faith.

December 1944 Corrie was released two weeks after Betsie's death.

As soon as Corrie came back home, she made it her mission to help all the people who had suffered from the war, as well as sharing her story with thousands of people around the world.

Corrie taught us to trust God in every situation and to find in him the strength to forgive, even when it's really hard.

NORTH
AMERICA

The Netherlands

Germany

SOUTH
AMERICA

World Map

Where in the world
did Corrie's story
take place?

ASIA

AUSTRALIA

Interact With Corrie's Story!

's

Family Project: The Netherlands

God did amazing things through Corrie ten Boom all around the world and right where she lived: the Netherlands! As you learn about the Netherlands, take time to pray for the Christians there and the people who don't yet know about Jesus! Read and discuss Matthew 28 v 16–20 and Revelation 7 v 9–11 together to learn about God's heart for all peoples.

Day 1: Overview

- Locate the Netherlands on a globe or map.
- How many people live in the Netherlands?

- Look up pictures of the Netherlands.

Day 2: Food

- What is a typical meal in the Netherlands?

- What are some popular snacks?

- If you can, make a Dutch meal together.

Day 3: Culture

- What are some of the holidays celebrated in the Netherlands?

- ...ead an overview of the history of the Netherlands.
- ...at makes up traditional Dutch clothing?

...oys & Games

- ...ort of toys are popular in the Netherlands?

- What games do children in the Netherlands like to play?

- What is school like in the Netherlands?

Day 5: Religion & Missions

- What are the primary religions in the Netherlands?

- How many Christians are in the Netherlands?

- Are there unreached people groups in the Netherlands?

- What are church services like in the Netherlands?

4-7s

All About

Corrie ten Boom

By: _____

My Drawing of Corrie ten Boom

Where did Corrie grow up?

When was Corrie born?

What kind of shop did Corrie's family own?

What Did Corrie Do When...
Circle the Answer

Jewish People Were Hurt — Asked God to Use Her to Help Them **OR** Moved Away from the War

She Was in Prison — Played Games **OR** Read the Bible

She Was Freed — Told People about Jesus **OR** Became a Singer

Jews Needed to Hide — Told Them to Leave **OR** Built a Secret Room for Them

1

8-11s

Biography Report for

Corrie ten Boom

By: _____

My favorite thing about Corrie:

_____

Person from the Bible Corrie reminds me of:

_____

A question I would ask Corrie:

_____

Three words I would use to describe Corrie:

1. _____
2. _____
3. _____

Remember this Verse Corrie Loved

"You _____ my _____; I _____ in and _____"

Psalm 119 v 114

Can you say it 5 times without looking?

· PASS·

Corrie ten Boom

Year of Birth:

Hometown:

Job Title:

Search Online to Find:
Ask an adult about doing this together!

When was World War 2? Who was fighting?

How many Jewish people did Corrie and her family help? How did they help?

What did Corrie do after the war ended? Where did she go?

1

Download Free Resources at

thegoodbook.com/kids-resources

Do Great Things for God

Inspiring Biographies for Young Children

Corrie ten Boom
The Courageous Woman and the Secret Room
Laura Caputo-Wickham
Illustrated by Isabel Muñoz

Betsey Stockton
The Girl With a Missionary Dream
Laura Caputo-Wickham
Illustrated by Eunji Jung

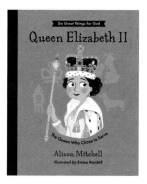

Queen Elizabeth II
The Queen Who Chose to Serve
Alison Mitchell
Illustrated by Emma Randall

Helen Roseveare
The Doctor Who Kept Going No Matter What
Laura Caputo-Wickham
Illustrated by Cecilia Messina

Gladys Aylward
The Little Woman With a Big Dream
Laura Caputo-Wickham
Illustrated by Jess Rose

Betty Greene
The Girl Who Longed to Fly
Laura Caputo-Wickham
Illustrated by Héloïse Mab

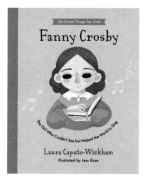

Fanny Crosby
The Girl Who Couldn't See but Helped the World to Sing
Laura Caputo-Wickham
Illustrated by Jess Rose

Fannie Lou Hamer
The Courageous Woman Who Marched for Dignity
K. A. Ellis
Illustrated by Shin Maeng

Maria Fearing
The Girl Who Dreamed of Distant Lands
K. A. Ellis
Illustrated by Isabel Muñoz

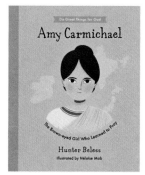

Amy Carmichael
The Brown-eyed Girl Who Learned to Pray
Hunter Beless
Illustrated by Héloïse Mab

Susannah Spurgeon
The Pastor's Wife Who Didn't Let Sickness Stop Her
Mary K. Mohler
Illustrated by Cecilia Messina